Kids' Guide to Learning the UKULELE

Kids' Guide to Learning the UKULELE

24 Songs to Learn and Play

By Emily Arrow

Photography by Alex Crawford

A Special Thank You to Kala Brand Ukulele

Happy Fox BOOKS

© 2020 by Emily Arrow and Happy Fox Books, an imprint of Fox Chapel Publishing Company, Inc., 903 Square Street, Mount Joy, PA 17552.

Kids' Guide to Learning the Ukulele is an original work, first published in 2020 by Fox Chapel Publishing Company, Inc. Reproduction of its contents is strictly prohibited without written permission from the rights holder.

ISBN 978-1-64124-048-2

Project Team
Technical Reviewer: Mika McDougall
Editors: Jeremy Hauck, Laura Taylor
Cover design: Llara Pazdan, David Fisk
Interior page design: Llara Pazdan
Indexer: Jay Kreider

Library of Congress Control Number:2019953931

To learn more about the other great books from Fox Chapel Publishing, or to find a retailer near you, call toll-free 800-457-9112 or visit us at *www.FoxChapelPublishing.com*.

We are always looking for talented authors. To submit an idea, please send a brief inquiry to acquisitions@foxchapelpublishing.com.

Fox Chapel Publishing makes every effort to use environmentally friendly paper for printing.

Printed in China
Fourth printing

Hello! Hello!

I'm Emily Arrow. I create songs, stories, and YouTube videos with my ukulele named Bow (get it? Like bow and "Arrow"!). Being a musician is my way of learning more about myself and sharing who I am with the world. I love performing with my ukulele at theaters, libraries, bookstores, and radio stations to share my music with kids all over the country.

Why am I so obsessed with the ukulele?

I started playing the piano when I was seven years old . . . but it was not very easy for me! I already loved to sing, so my goal was to sing and play songs on the piano. I was impatient and wanted to learn faster. If you have ever been impatient with something you really wanted, you will understand what I mean.

But no matter what, something inside me knew I wanted to make music. Plunking out my own song, singing, and even reading my music lesson books — these were things I knew I wanted to do for the rest of my life.

So after a few more years of piano lessons (with my *very* patient piano teacher) I was finally able to write, sing, and play my own songs. Now zoom ahead to me at music school. I felt so lucky to be studying music every single day in college! I was still playing the piano until one day at lunch when my friend brought his ukulele.

He asked me, "Have you ever tried playing the ukulele?" I quietly imagined myself trying to learn another instrument. I expected it would probably be as frustrating, long, and challenging as learning the piano had been. But then my friend suggested a trade: "I'll trade you a ukulele lesson for a burrito!" Deal.

While we ate lunch together, I learned to play my four favorite dot chords: **C** **F** **G** and **Am** .

And you're in luck because we'll learn each of these chords in this guide. Since most songs can be played using only a few ukulele chords, it only took a couple of weeks for me to be able to sing along—just like it will for you.

Then after I spent time teaching music in Hawaii, I began to understand a lot more about the uke.

Friends of all ages shared their passion for this magical Hawaiian instrument—including how to correctly pronounce *ukulele* (oo-koo-lay-lay)!

Now whether I'm performing, making a YouTube video, or even writing a story, I always have my favorite instrument in hand—my ukulele. And I'm so excited to help you learn to play the ukulele too. Are you ready to strum along?

ooo-koo-lay-lay

Table of Contents

24 Songs
to Learn & Play

About the Ukulele

How Do You Say *Ukulele?*

Maybe you're used to pronouncing *ukulele* as, "YOU-koo-LAY-lee." But in this book, we'll pronounce *ukulele* like this:

ooo-koo-lay-lay

CHALLENGE!
Say it like this.
10 times. Super fast!

Ukulele Sizes

There are a few different ukulele sizes; here are the most common types. They're all fun! Do you know which size your ukulele is?

soprano

concert

tenor

Parts of the Ukulele

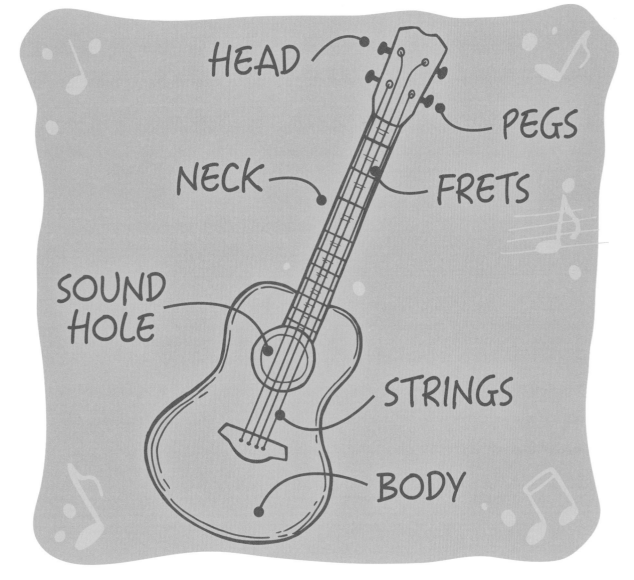

HEAD

PEGS

NECK

FRETS

SOUND HOLE

STRINGS

BODY

Name Your Ukulele

Because instruments are an important part of our lives, it's fun to give an instrument their own name. What could you name your own ukulele? Maybe name it after a favorite character, animal, or food. For example, I named one of my ukuleles "Avocado the Ukulele"!

◇ ◦ ◇ ◦ ◇ ◦ ◇ ◦ ◇ ◦ ◇ ◦ ◇ ◦ ◇ ◦ ◇ ◦

WHAT IS YOUR UKULELE'S NAME?

◇ ◦ ◇ ◦ ◇ ◦ ◇ ◦ ◇ ◦ ◇ ◦ ◇ ◦ ◇ ◦ ◇ ◦

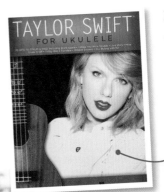

UKULELES ARE AWESOME.

YOU'VE PROBABLY SEEN UKULELES ALL OVER THE PLACE LATELY—AND THAT'S BECAUSE THEY ARE!

Popular ukulele musicians like Jake Shimabukuro and artists such as Zooey Deschanel, Taylor Swift, and Vance Joy are writing and performing on the ukulele. Now it's your turn to play too, so let's get started.

Taylor Swift has been playing ukulele for many years. There is even a ukulele songbook of her songs.

How to Hold Your Ukulele

It helps to sit down on a chair or cross-legged on the floor while you're learning to play.
Be sure to sit up straight.

RIGHT ARM:

Hand above
the sound hole
to strum

Fingers make
a "pinch" shape
to strum

LEFT ARM:

Hand wraps
around the back
of the neck

Thumb rests
around the back

1, 2, 3, and pinky
fingers curl down
on the strings

The fingers we'll use each have a number.

Tuning

Each string has its own number. When you're holding your uke, the string closest to your eyes is string 4. Then 3, 2, and 1 follow.

To tune our ukuleles, we assign each string a pitch. And each pitch has a **letter name**. Once we tune each string to its letter name, we can learn to play songs!

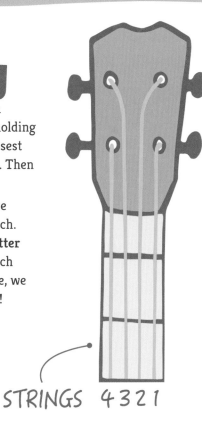

STRINGS 4 3 2 1

FUN FACT

If you wanted to, you could tune all of the strings to the EXACT SAME NOTE! That's because each string can be made higher or lower by twisting the tuning pegs.

ARE YOU WONDERING WHAT THESE ARE?

Tuning pegs are little knobs for twisting the strings. When we twist the string tighter or looser, we **tune** our ukulele. **Tuning** is twisting each string to a different **pitch**, or musical note.

Tuning Each String to G-C-E-A

Can you follow each string with your fingers from the **sound hole**, up to the **peg** it's attached to?

Here's a funny way to remember each string's letter names for tuning: **Good Cats Eat Apples**.

CATS   EAT

GOOD   APPLES

STRINGS 4 3 2 1

Each string will sound higher or lower than another, just like in the illustration!

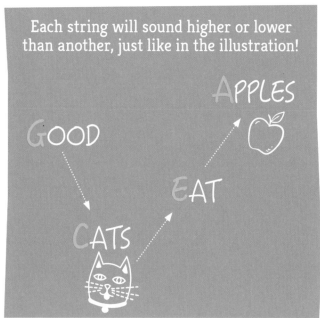

APPLES

GOOD

EAT

CATS

Let's Tune Up

The simplest way to tune is with an electronic tuning device or app.

To get started, put your **left hand** on the tuning peg connected to **string 4**, the string we want to tune to the musical pitch **G**.

Then your **right hand** will **keep plucking string 4** while you twist the tuning peg.

◆◇◆◇◆◇◆◇◆◇◆◇◆◇◆◇◆◇◆

How to tune:

Twist the tuning peg to change the pitch of each string and repeatedly **pluck** the string to hear how it sounds. It's tuned when the ukulele string matches the sound of its musical letter on the electronic device or app!

◆◇◆◇◆◇◆◇◆◇◆◇◆◇◆◇◆◇◆◇

Which direction to twist:

For strings **4 and 3**, twist **to the sky** to make it **sound high!** *(twist left or counterclockwise)*

For strings **2 and 1**, twist **to the ground** to make a **high sound!** *(twist right or clockwise)*

Pro Tips for Tuning

1. If you end up too far away from the letter you're trying to match, try twisting the peg in the opposite direction.

2. If a string sounds WAY too low or WAY too high, ask a teacher or musician for help getting the string back to a middle place so you can try tuning again.

3. Tuning is one of the hardest parts of learning to play an instrument with strings. Be kind to yourself when it's tricky and takes longer than you expected. You've got this! Even musicians who have been tuning for many years still take their time.

When Should You Tune?

- Each time you play your ukulele
- In between playing songs
- If your ukulele sounds out of tune

Strumming

To **strum,** your right hand makes a **pinch shape** with the fingers and thumb touching.

A **down strum** is when we strum downward (from string 4 to string 1).

Starting with the pinch shape, the fingernail of your first finger will be what touches the strings to make a noise. Some people prefer to strum with their thumb instead, and that's okay too!

Strumming down on the tuned strings makes a musical sound. Sing or speak the words to your own tune.

DOWN STRUM

Down Strum Song

Count-in slowly: 1, 2, here we go!

Words to Sing or Speak	Strum
Down strum once	↓
Down strum twice	↓
Down strum song	↓
Does sound nice!	↓

REPEAT RAINBOW

When you see the repeat rainbow at the end of a song, it means to play the song again. You can repeat the song as many times as you want to.

WHEN YOU PLAY UKULELE, GO WITH THE FLOW.

YOU CAN DECIDE HOW THE SONG WILL GO!

Dot Chords

Your Left Hand

To make different sounds on the ukulele, you'll **press your left fingers down on the neck in between the frets.** When you press down on a string, it changes the pitch of the string because, in a way, it makes the string's length different. So, then the pitch changes to be higher or lower!

To press on the fretboard and make a sound, curl your fingers round like spiders, not flat like pancakes. Then press in between the frets, not ON the frets.

Notice that my short fingernails let my fingertips push down on the strings in between the frets more easily! Over time, the fingers on your left hand will get stronger and be able to play shapes with ease, so it's important to keep practicing to develop finger strength.

Try pressing down using your finger strength on the 4th string in between two of the frets.

If you can't hear the note change from how it sounded before you pressed on the string or hear buzzing sounds, it probably means you aren't pressing hard enough. And if your fingertips start hurting too much, you might be pressing too hard!

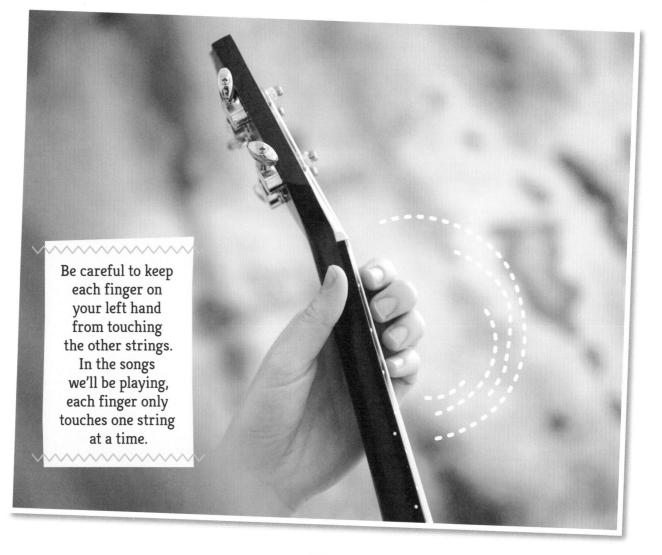

Be careful to keep each finger on your left hand from touching the other strings. In the songs we'll be playing, each finger only touches one string at a time.

Forming Chords

When your left hand makes a specific shape in between the **frets** (the lines on the neck) and you play multiple notes at the same time, we call that a chord! **Dot chords** show you where your left-hand fingers go on the frets. You can try using stickers like mine in the photos (available at office supply stores). If you don't have stickers, you can imagine the colors on the fretboard to help you play.

FUN FACT

Playing ukelele music is a great way to pass the time. That's what astronaut Neil Armstrong did while waiting to go home after his space flight. He walked on the moon in 1969—the first person to ever do that!

24 Songs
to Learn & Play

How to sing the songs while you strum:

🎸 sing the tune if you know it

or

🎸 create your own way of singing the words

or

🎸 speak the words

or

🎸 any combination of singing and speaking

LISTEN FIRST!
If you don't know the songs in this book, visit www.EmilyArrow.com/LearningUkulele to hear each one. Listening to the tune first will help you learn how to play the songs!

The Red Dot (C Chord) Song

Here's where the red dot (C) sticker goes on the fretboard of your ukulele.

Put the third finger of your left hand on the red dot to make a C Chord shape. Remember: Your finger will be **in between** the second and third fret, **not** ON the fret.

STRING	FINGER	FRET
1st string	3rd finger	3rd fret

The Red Dot (C Chord) Song

Make the C Chord shape with your left hand and push down gently on the string to hold the chord shape. Strum when you see the ⒸC and sing or speak the words to the song while you play!

INTRODUCTION			
C	C	C	C
1	2	3	4
⬇	⬇	⬇	⬇

SINGALONG			
C	C	C	C
Red	dot,	C	chord
⬇	⬇	⬇	⬇
C	C	C	C
1	2	3	4
⬇	⬇	⬇	⬇
C	C	C	C
Red	dot,	C	chord
⬇	⬇	⬇	⬇
C	C	C	C
1	2	3	4
⬇	⬇	⬇	⬇

Row, Row, Row Your Boat

Guess what? The song "Row, Row, Row Your Boat" uses only one chord! Keep a steady down strum going while you strum **C** and don't forget to singalong.

TIP:

The fingertips on your left hand might start to get sore or even get calluses. It's ok if this happens! Always feel free to take a break from practicing for a few days.

CHALLENGE

Try playing "Row, Row, Row Your Boat" at different speeds.

1st time: medium speed   **3rd time:** very slowly

2nd time: super fast   **4th time:** medium speed again

Row, Row, Row Your Boat

INTRODUCTION			
C	C	C	C
1	2	3	4
⬇	⬇	⬇	⬇

SINGALONG			
C	C	C	C
Row,	row,	row your	boat
⬇	⬇	⬇	⬇
C	C	C	C
Gently	down the	stream	
⬇	⬇	⬇	⬇
C	C	C	C
Merrily,	merrily,	merrily,	merrily
⬇	⬇	⬇	⬇
C	C	C	C
Life is	but a	dream.	
⬇	⬇	⬇	⬇

Find-the-Sock Game

How to Play

For this song and game, you'll need a partner and a sock to hide! If you're the one strumming the ukulele during the game, you are the "hider" of the sock. The person listening for clues is the "seeker."

1. The seeker closes their eyes.

2. The hider quickly hides the sock and gets ready to play ukulele.

3. The hider plays **C** over and over to give the seeker clues of how close or far they are from the hidden sock.

   playing softly = the sock is still far away

   playing loudly = the sock is close

4. Once your partner finds the sock, try teaching him or her **C** so you can take turns hiding and seeking!

FUN FACT

Millions of ukuleles were sold in the 1920s in the United States. Everyone wanted to learn how to play the cool instrument from the Hawaiian islands.

The Yellow Dot (F Chord) Song

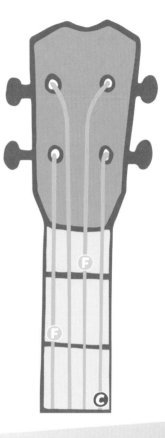

Here's where the Yellow Dot (F) stickers go on the fretboard of your ukulele.

STRING	FINGER	FRET
4th string	2nd finger	2nd fret
2nd string	1st finger	1st fret

The Yellow Dot (F) Chord uses the left-hand fingers 1 and 2, or "bunny ear fingers." Now press fingers 1 and 2 on the yellow dots to make an F Chord shape!

The Yellow Dot (F Chord) Song

Make the F Chord shape with your left hand and strum when you see the (F). Sing or speak along with your ukulele.

INTRODUCTION			
(F)	(F)	(F)	(F)
1	2	3	4
⇩	⇩	⇩	⇩

SINGALONG			
(F)	(F)	(F)	(F)
F	chord,	yel-	low
⇩	⇩	⇩	⇩
(F)	(F)	(F)	(F)
I	feel	mel-	low!
⇩	⇩	⇩	⇩

ROCKSTAR ENDING!

How? Strum ⇩⇧⇩⇧ super fast.
Like a rock star.

Shhh!

Let's use both chords we've learned so far in this song: **F** and **C**. Sing or speak the words to your own tune!

When you see this symbol, **pat your ukulele** with your right hand over the strings. This will stop the sound and make a light **pat** sound to keep the beat.

Shhh!

INTRODUCTION			
C	C	F	F
1	2	3	4
⬇	⬇	⬇	⬇

SINGALONG			
C	C	F	
Red	red	yellow	shh!
⬇	⬇	⬇	👏
F	F	C	
Yellow	yellow	red	shh!
⬇	⬇	⬇	👏
C	C	F	
Red	red	yellow	shh!
⬇	⬇	⬇	👏
F	F	C	
Slee-	py	head.	Wake up!
⬇	⬇	⬇	👏

The 10-Second Challenge

Start with your left hand on **C** without strumming. You won't need your right hand to strum at all for this challenge.

Count from 1 to 10 and switch from chords **C** to **F** like this:

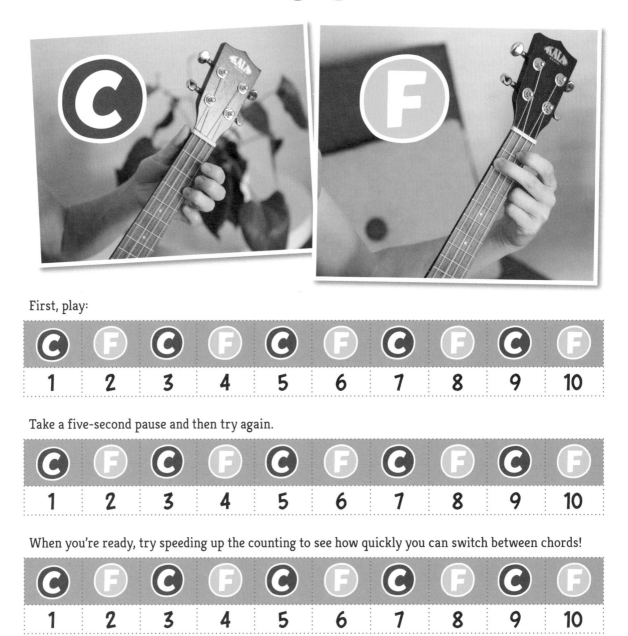

First, play:

C	**F**	**C**	**F**	**C**	**F**	**C**	**F**	**C**	**F**
1	2	3	4	5	6	7	8	9	10

Take a five-second pause and then try again.

C	**F**	**C**	**F**	**C**	**F**	**C**	**F**	**C**	**F**
1	2	3	4	5	6	7	8	9	10

When you're ready, try speeding up the counting to see how quickly you can switch between chords!

C	**F**	**C**	**F**	**C**	**F**	**C**	**F**	**C**	**F**
1	2	3	4	5	6	7	8	9	10

Practice is fun!

The Green Dot (G Chord) Song

Here's where the Green Dot G stickers go on the fretboard of your ukulele.

STRING	FINGER	FRET
2nd string	3rd finger	3rd fret
1st string	2nd finger	2nd fret
3rd string	1st finger	2nd fret

Put fingers 1, 2, and 3 on the green dots to make a G Chord shape. Your fingers might feel like they're crossing each other to find a dot to land on, and that's nothing to worry about. It's part of the fun to see how quickly your fingers can memorize the G Chord! The Green Dot G Chord is a challenging chord shape because we'll use three fingers. Hang in there! It will get easier each time you practice.

38

The Green Dot (G Chord) Song

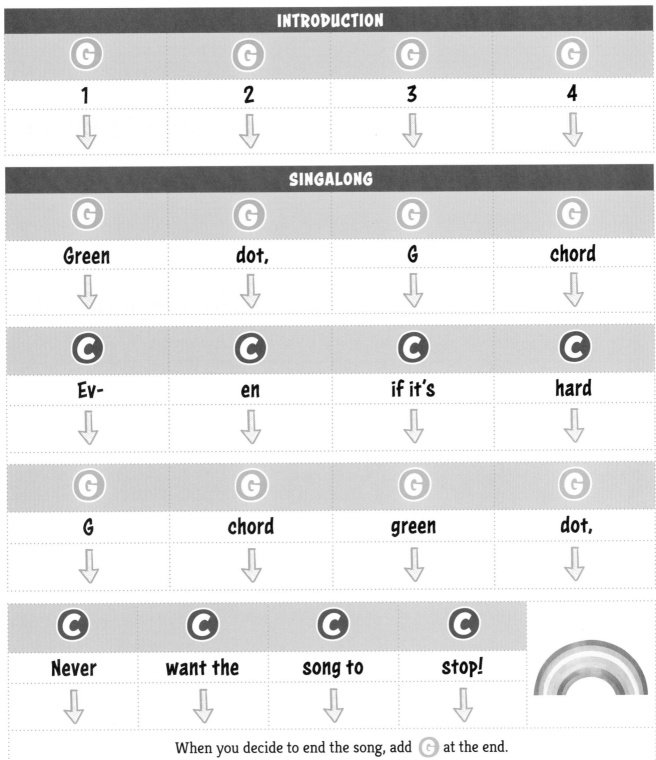

INTRODUCTION

G	G	G	G
1	2	3	4
⇩	⇩	⇩	⇩

SINGALONG

G	G	G	G
Green	dot,	G	chord
⇩	⇩	⇩	⇩

C	C	C	C
Ev-	en	if it's	hard
⇩	⇩	⇩	⇩

G	G	G	G
G	chord	green	dot,
⇩	⇩	⇩	⇩

C	C	C	C
Never	want the	song to	stop!
⇩	⇩	⇩	⇩

When you decide to end the song, add G at the end.

39

The Itsy Bitsy Spider

Try this familiar song that uses all the chords you've learned so far. Before you begin, can you find the spots in the song where you'll play the G Chord?

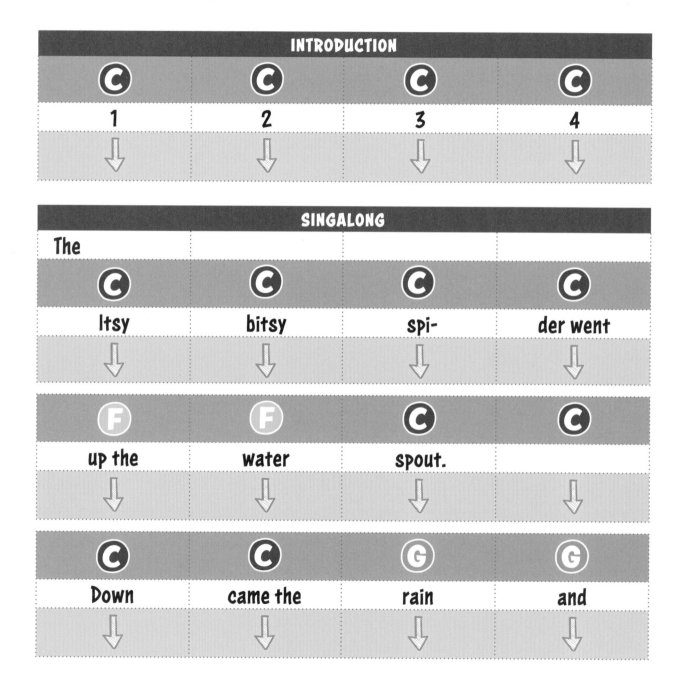

F	**F**	**C**	**C**
washed the	spider	out.	
⬇	⬇	⬇	⬇

C	**C**	**C**	**C**
Out	came the	sun	and
⬇	⬇	⬇	⬇

F	**F**	**C**	**C**
dried up	all the	rain	and the
⬇	⬇	⬇	⬇

C	**C**	**C**	**C**
Itsy	bitsy	spi-	der went
⬇	⬇	⬇	⬇

F	**G**	**C**	**C**
up the	spout a-	gain!	
⬇	⬇	⬇	⬇

Let's Read a Book
(to the tune of "Skip to My Lou")

I LOVE reading. In fact, I even love to sing songs about books. Here's a song you might already know, so I've added some new lyrics—about books!

INTRODUCTION			
C	C	C	C
1	2	3	4
⬇	⬇	⬇	⬇

SINGALONG			
C	C	C	C
Let's,	let's,	let's read a	book,
(Lou,	lou	skip to my	lou,)
⬇	⬇	⬇	⬇
G	G	G	G
Let's,	let's,	let's read a	book,
(Lou,	lou	skip to my	lou,)
⬇	⬇	⬇	⬇
C	C	C	C
Let's,	let's,	let's read a	book,
(Lou,	lou	skip to my	lou,)
⬇	⬇	⬇	⬇
F	G	C	C
Let's read a	book of	mu-	sic.
(Skip to my	lou my	dar-	ling.)
⬇	⬇	⬇	⬇

If You Want to Play Ukulele
(to the tune of "My Bonnie Lies Over The Ocean")

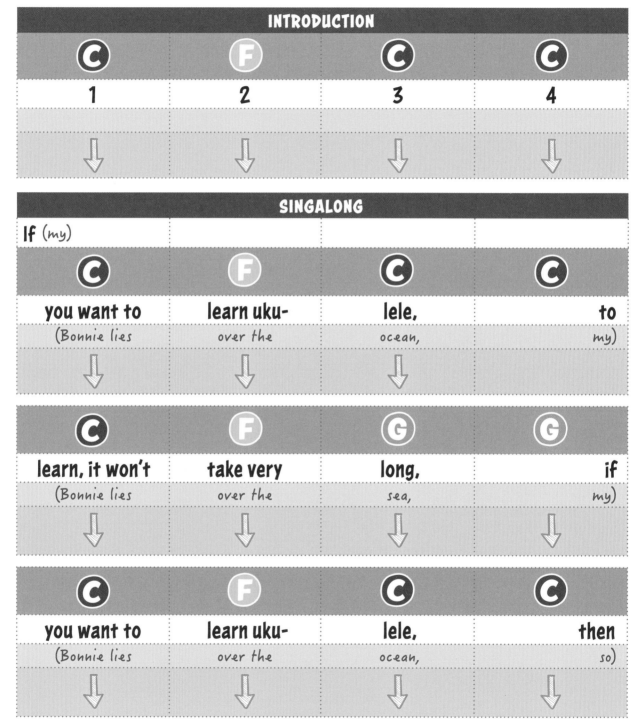

INTRODUCTION

C	F	C	C
1	2	3	4
⬇	⬇	⬇	⬇

SINGALONG

If (my)

C	F	C	C
you want to	learn uku-	lele,	to
(Bonnie lies	over the	ocean,	my)
⬇	⬇	⬇	

C	F	G	G
learn, it won't	take very	long,	if
(Bonnie lies	over the	sea,	my)
⬇	⬇	⬇	⬇

C	F	C	C
you want to	learn uku-	lele,	then
(Bonnie lies	over the	ocean,	so)
⬇	⬇	⬇	⬇

F	**G**	**C**	**C**
just play a-	long with the	song!	
(Bring back my	Bonnie to	me!)	
⬇	⬇	⬇	⬇

C	**C**	**F**	**F**
Red,	red,	yellow,	yellow,
(Bring,	back,	bring,	back,)
⬇	⬇	⬇	⬇

G	**G**	**C**	**C**
Green,	green,	red	again!
(Bring,	back to,	me to	me!)
⬇	⬇	⬇	⬇

C	**C**	**F**	**F**
Red,	red,	yellow,	yellow,
(Bring,	back,	bring,	back,)
⬇	⬇	⬇	⬇

G	**G**	**C**	**C**
Green,	green,	red	again!
(Bring,	back to,	me to	me!)
⬇	⬇	⬇	⬇

Mary Had a Little Uke
(to the tune of "Mary Had a Little Lamb")

Instead of a little lamb, Mary had a . . . little uke! This song has verses, or new lyrics each time you sing. To sing verse 1, you'll sing the lyrics on the top line. Then verse 2 and 3.

INTRODUCTION			
C	F	C	C
1	2	3	4
⬇	⬇	⬇	⬇

SINGALONG			
C	F	C	C
1. Mary	had a	little	uke,
(Mary	had a	little	lamb,)
2. Every-	where that	Mary	went,
3. It followed	her to	school one	day,
⬇	⬇	⬇	⬇
G	G	C	C
1. little	uke,	little	uke,
(little	lamb,	little	lamb,)
2. Mary	went,	Mary	went,
3. School one	day,	school one	day,
⬇	⬇	⬇	⬇

C	F	C	C
1. Mary	had a	little	uke,
(Mary	had a	little	lamb,)
2. Every-	where that	Mary	went,
3. When it	went to	school one	day,
⬇	⬇	⬇	⬇

G	G	C	
1. and played it	all the	time.	
(its fleece was	white as	snow.)	
2. Her uke was	sure to	go.	
3. they told her	uke ,	"hello!"	
⬇	⬇	⬇	

London Bridge

"London Bridge" might be a familiar song to you. Try writing your own lyrics on the next page. Try to rhyme the last words in each line.

WRITE YOUR OWN LYRICS!

INTRODUCTION			
C	C	C	C
1	2	3	4
⬇	⬇	⬇	⬇

SINGALONG			
C	C	C	C
(London	Bridge is	falling	down,)
⬇	⬇	⬇	⬇
G	G	C	C
(falling	down,	falling	down,)
⬇	⬇	⬇	⬇
C	C	C	C
(London	Bridge is	falling	down,)
⬇	⬇	⬇	⬇
F	G	C	C
(My	fair	la-	dy.)
⬇	⬇	⬇	⬇

Swee-dee-dee
(to the tune of "Three Blind Mice")

This time, we'll have to switch from **C** to **G** very quickly for a fun song about snacks! At the end, say out loud something you'd like to eat for a snack. So, each verse, instead of singing swee-dee-dee, sing the three-beat snack or food that you love to eat. Like toast-and-jam!

SINGALONG			
C	**G**	**C**	
Swee	**dee**	**dee**	
(Three	blind	mice)	
(Straw-	ber-	ries)	
(Toast	and	jam)	
⬇	⬇	⬇	👏
C	**G**	**C**	
Swee	**dee**	**dee**	
(Three	blind	mice)	
⬇	⬇	⬇	👏
C	**G**	**C**	
What	**will we**	**eat?**	
(See	how they	run)	
⬇	⬇	⬇	👏

C	G	C	
What	**will we**	**eat?**	
(See	how they	run)	
⬇	⬇	⬇	👏

Old MacDonald Played a Strum
(to the tune of "Old MacDonald")

Notice: There are a few spots where the dot chords are closer to each other than before.
That means you'll play them **double the speed**. Try this pattern to practice:

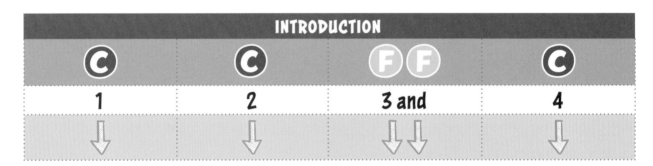

C	C	F F	C
(slow)	(slow)	(fast fast)	(slow)
⬇	⬇	⬇ ⬇	⬇

INTRODUCTION			
C	C	F F	C
1	2	3 and	4
⬇	⬇	⬇ ⬇	⬇

SINGALONG			
C	C	F F	C
Old Mac-	Donald	played a	strum,
(Old Mac-	Donald	had a	farm)
⬇	⬇	⬇ ⬇	⬇

C	G	C F	C
ee-yi,	ee-yi	o!	With a
(ee-yi,	ee-yi,	o!)	(With a)
⬇	⬇	⬇ ⬇	⬇

FUN FACT

1893's World's Columbian Exposition in Chicago saw the first major performance of Hawaiian music with ukulele.

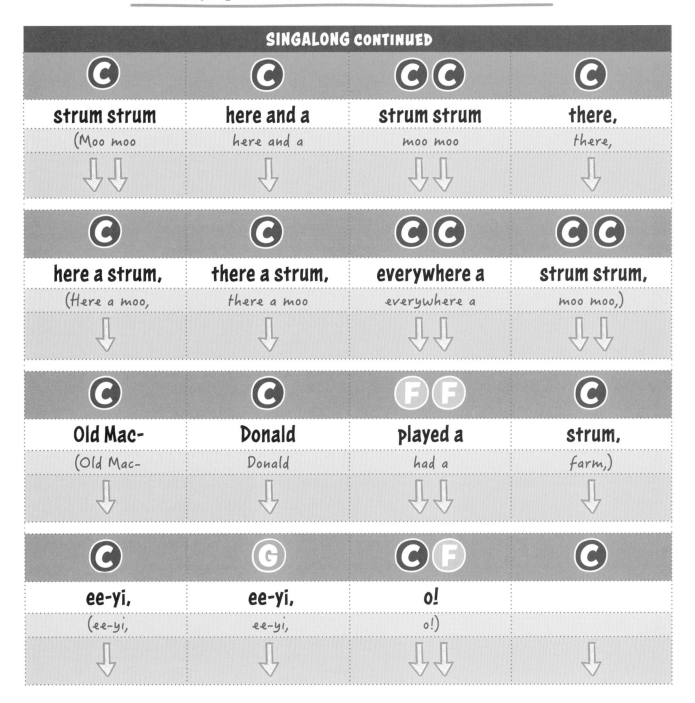

SINGALONG CONTINUED			
C	**C**	**C** **C**	**C**
strum strum	**here and a**	**strum strum**	**there,**
(Moo moo	here and a	moo moo	there,
C	**C**	**C** **C**	**C** **C**
here a strum,	**there a strum,**	**everywhere a**	**strum strum,**
(Here a moo,	there a moo	everywhere a	moo moo,)
C	**C**	**F** **F**	**C**
Old Mac-	**Donald**	**played a**	**strum,**
(Old Mac-	Donald	had a	farm,)
C	**G**	**C** **F**	**C**
ee-yi,	**ee-yi,**	**o!**	
(ee-yi,	ee-yi,	o!)	

Twinkle, Twinkle, Little Star

You probably know this song too, so we're going to learn it first—then try new lyrics on our next song. The strumming pattern changes at one part of the song. Can you see where it changes? When you look at the whole song before you start playing, you'll be more prepared!

INTRODUCTION			
C C	**C C**	**C C**	**C**
1 and	2 and	3 and	4
⬇⬇	⬇⬇	⬇⬇	⬇

SINGALONG			
C C	**C C**	**F F**	**C**
Twinkle,	twinkle,	lit-tle	star
⬇⬇	⬇⬇	⬇⬇	⬇
F F	**C C**	**G G**	**C**
How I	wonder	what you	are.
⬇⬇	⬇⬇	⬇⬇	⬇
C C	**F F**	**C C**	**G**
Up a-	bove the	world so	high,
⬇⬇	⬇⬇	⬇⬇	⬇

C C	F F	C C	G
Like a	dia-mond	in the	sky

C C	C C	F F	C
Twinkle,	twinkle,	lit-tle	star

F F	C C	G G	C
How I	wonder	what you	are.

Yoga-lele (to the tune of "Twinkle, Twinkle, Little Star")

Using the first half of the tune to "Twinkle, Twinkle, Little Star," let's do some yoga!

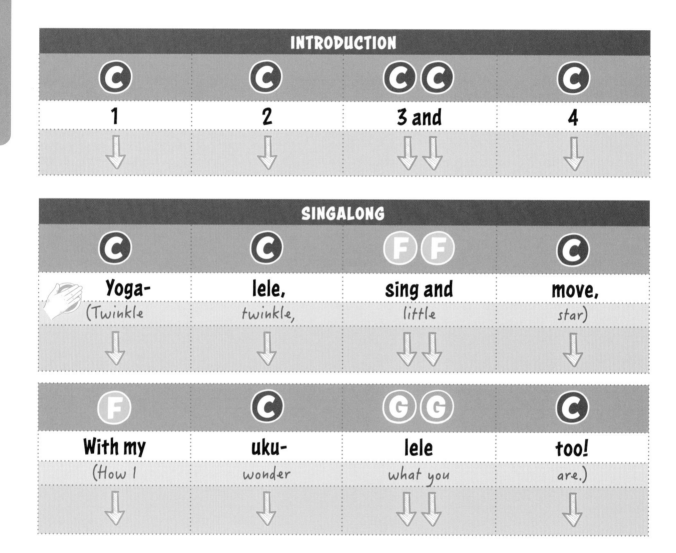

INTRODUCTION

C	C	C C	C
1	2	3 and	4
⬇	⬇	⬇ ⬇	⬇

SINGALONG

C	C	F F	C
Yoga- (Twinkle	lele, twinkle,	sing and little	move, star)
⬇	⬇	⬇ ⬇	⬇

F	C	G G	C
With my (How I	uku- wonder	lele what you	too! are.)
⬇	⬇	⬇ ⬇	⬇

Try each yoga pose below and **take four calm breaths** in and out. Make sure you have plenty of room so your ukulele stays safe while you stretch with it!

Down-Up

Now that we can strum down, let's try strumming UP too!

A **Down-Up strum** is when we drag our pinched, shaped left hand through the strings on the way back up from a down strum. Either the padded part of your first finger or your thumb's fingernail will touch the strings to make a sound. Try both ways and see which you prefer.

Down-Up strum

Down

Up

60

Try these **Down-Up** patterns to practice.

Pattern 1

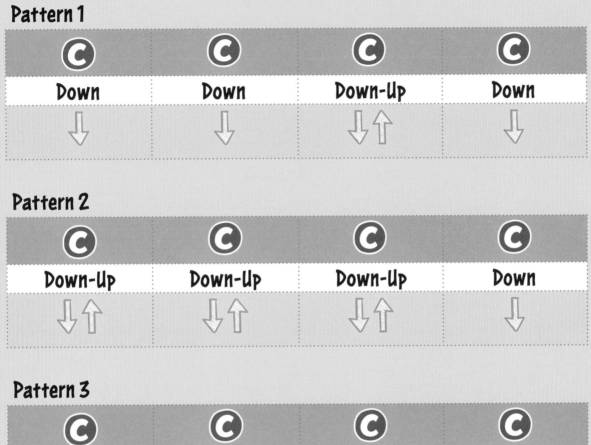

C	C	C	C
Down	Down	Down-Up	Down
⬇	⬇	⬇⬆	⬇

Pattern 2

C	C	C	C
Down-Up	Down-Up	Down-Up	Down
⬇⬆	⬇⬆	⬇⬆	⬇

Pattern 3

C	C	C	C
Down	Down-Up	Down	Down-Up
⬇	⬇⬆	⬇	⬇⬆

Pattern 4

C	C	C	C
Down	Down	Down	Down-Up
⬇	⬇	⬇	⬇⬆

Just Keep Strumming
(to the tune of "Frère Jacques")

What should you do if you miss a chord or mess up? You might want to start the whole song over . . . but try to keep going until you reach the end of the song!

Practice the new strumming pattern before beginning the song on page 64.

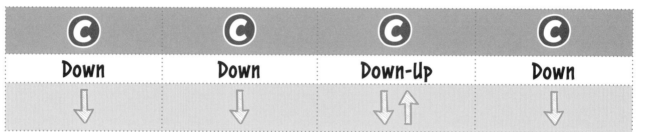

C	C	C	C
Down	Down	Down-Up	Down
⬇	⬇	⬇⬆	⬇

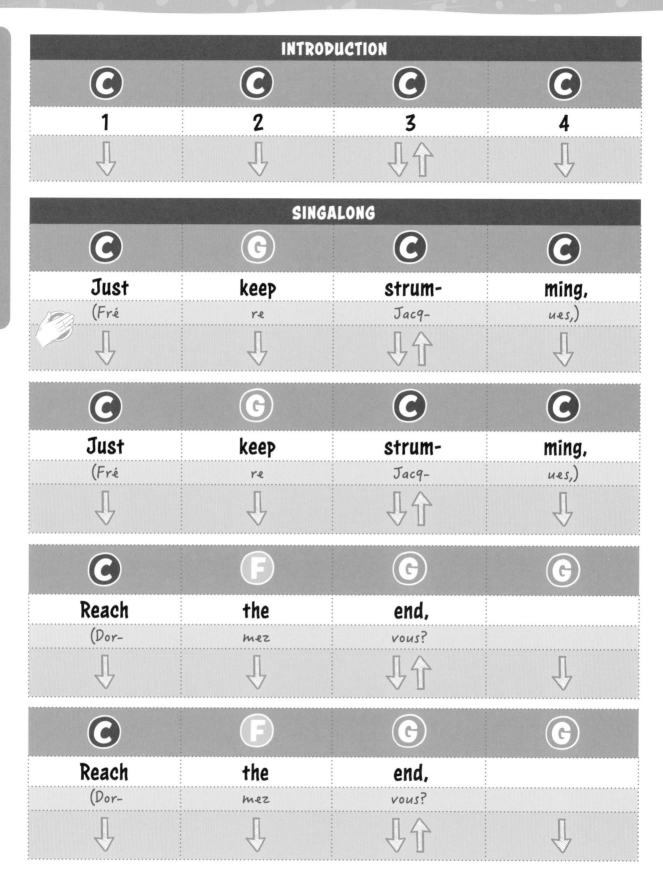

INTRODUCTION

C	C	C	C
1	2	3	4
↓	↓	↓↑	↓

SINGALONG

C	G	C	C
Just	keep	strum-	ming,
(Fré	re	Jacq-	ues,)
↓	↓	↓↑	↓

C	G	C	C
Just	keep	strum-	ming,
(Fré	re	Jacq-	ues,)
↓	↓	↓↑	↓

C	F	G	G
Reach	the	end,	
(Dor-	mez	vous?	
↓	↓	↓↑	↓

C	F	G	G
Reach	the	end,	
(Dor-	mez	vous?	
↓	↓	↓↑	↓

C	G	C	C
Even	**when you**	**mess**	**up,**
(Morning	bells are	ring-	ing)
⬇	⬇	⬇⬆	⬇

C	G	C	C
You don't	**have to**	**give**	**up**
(Morning	bells are	ring-	ing)
⬇	⬇	⬇⬆	⬇

C	G	C	C
Try	**a-**	**gain.**	
(Ding	ding	dong.)	
⬇	⬇	⬇⬆	⬇

C	G	C	C
Try	**a-**	**gain.**	
(Ding	ding	dong.)	
⬇	⬇	⬇⬆	⬇

FUN FACT

The ukulele came from a small, guitar-like instrument called a machéte (pronounced "ma-CHET"). It was brought to Hawaii by sailors visiting from Portugal.

You Are My Sunshine

Have you heard this song before? It's one of my favorites to play on the uke. Since you probably already know how the song goes, it's time to try a more challenging strumming pattern. Practice the DOWN / DOWN-UP pattern below:

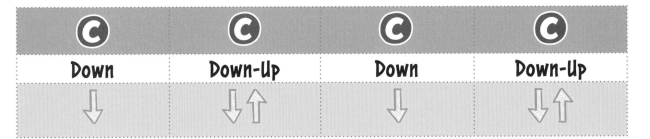

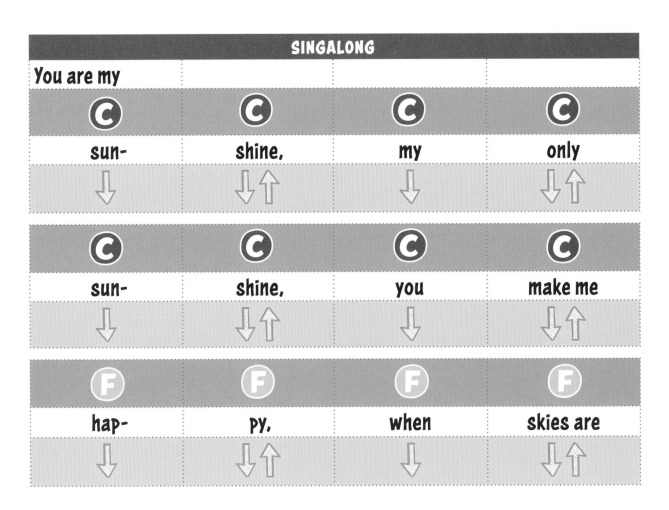

C	C	C	C
gray.		You'll	never
⬇	⬇⬆	⬇	⬇⬆

F	F	F	F
know,	dear,	how	much I
⬇	⬇⬆	⬇	⬇⬆

C	C	C	C
love	you.		Please don't
⬇	⬇⬆	⬇	⬇⬆

C	C	G	G
take	my	sun-	shine
⬇	⬇⬆	⬇	⬇⬆

C	F	C	
away.			
⬇	⬇⬆	⬇	

Aloha Means Hello
(to the tune of "The Farmer in the Dell")

Practice the DOWN/DOWN-UP pattern below:

C	C	C	C
Down	Down	Down-Up	Down
⬇	⬇	⬇⬆	⬇

Now practice with some of the words to "Farmer in the Dell," the tune of the song we're about to sing.

C	C	C	C
Farmer	in the	dell,	
⬇	⬇	⬇⬆	⬇

C	C	C	C
farmer	in the	dell,	
⬇	⬇	⬇⬆	⬇

FUN FACT
Some ukuleles have been made out of
wooden boxes and other items.

Count in slowly: 1, 2, here we go!

SINGALONG			
C	C	C	C
Aloha	**means**	**hello,**	
(The farmer	*in the*	*dell,)*	
⬇	⬇	⬇⬆	⬇
C	C	C	C
Aloha	**means**	**hello,**	
(The farmer	*in the*	*dell,)*	
⬇	⬇	⬇⬆	⬇
C	C	C	C
peaceful-	**ness and**	**happi-**	**ness,**
(heigh and	*ho,*	*the*	*derry, oh,)*
⬇	⬇	⬇⬆	⬇
C	G	C	C
Aloha	**means**	**hello!**	
(The farmer	*in the*	*dell.)*	
⬇	⬇	⬇⬆	⬇

The Blue Dot (A Minor Chord) Song

Here's where the Blue Dot **Am** stickers go on the fretboard of your ukulele.

The small **m** next to the letter A in Am stands for **minor**, which means it sounds dark or even sad.

The shape of the Blue Dot **Am** is similar to the Yellow Dot **F** Chord but with one less dot. Just like making an F Chord shape, your second finger will reach to the second fret of the first string. And that's it!

STRING	FINGER	FRET
4th string	2nd finger	2nd fret

The Blue Dot (A Minor Chord) Song

The Blue Dot Song is similar to the song "Rain, Rain, Go Away" to help you remember that the (Am) can sometimes sound blue, like a rainy day.

INTRODUCTION			
(Am)	(Am)	(Am)	(Am)
1	2	down-down	go!
⬇	⬇	⬇⬇	⬇

SINGALONG			
(Am)	(G)	(Am)	(Am)
Rain,	rain,	go a-	way,
⬇	⬇	⬇⬇	⬇
(Am)	(G)	(Am)	(Am)
(just strum)			
⬇	⬇	⬇⬇	⬇
(Am)	(G)	(Am)	(Am)
Blue	dot,	minor	A
⬇	⬇	⬇⬇	⬇
(Am)	(G)	(Am)	(Am)
(just strum)			
⬇	⬇	⬇⬇	⬇

Pumpkin, Pumpkin, Ghost!

The (Am) is fun to use because it can sound a bit spooky! Each time we sing the word *ghost*, we'll play the (Am) chord.

Notice: Strum twice when we sing the word *pumpkin* and only once when we sing the word *ghost*.

Count in slowly: 1, 2, ready, go!

SINGALONG			
(F)(F)	(F)(F)	(Am)	
Pump-kin	pump-kin	ghost!	Boo!
⇓⇓	⇓⇓	⇓	👏
(F)(F)	(F)(F)	(Am)	
Pump-kin	pump-kin	ghost!	Boo!
⇓⇓	⇓⇓	⇓	👏
(F)(F)	(F)(F)	(G)	(G)
pump-kins	on the	ground,	but the
⇓⇓	⇓⇓	⇓	⇓
(Am)(Am)	(Am)(Am)	(Am)	
ghost can-	not be	found.	Boo!
⇓	⇓⇓	⇓	👏

Do You Know the Switcheroo?
(to the tune of "Do You Know the Muffin Man?")

INTRODUCTION			
C	C	C	C
1	2	here we	go!
⬇	⬇	⬇⬆	⬇

SINGALONG			
C	C	C	C
Do you	know the	switch-	eroo,
(Do you	know the	muffin	man?)
⬇	⬇	⬇⬆	⬇
F	F	G	G
the switch-	eroo, the	switch-	eroo?
(The muffin	man, the	muffin	man?)
⬇	⬇	⬇⬆	⬇
C	C	C	C
Do you	know the	switch-	eroo,
(Do you	know the	muffin	man?)
⬇	⬇	⬇⬆	⬇

SINGALONG CONTINUED			
(G)	**(G)**	**(C)**	**(C)**
It goes	**just like**	**this,**	**hey!**
(Lives on	Drury	Lane,	hey!)
⬇	⬇	⬇	⬇

SPEAK THIS PART			
(C)	**(F)**	**(G)**	**(Am)**
Red	**yellow**	**green**	**blue**
⬇	⬇	⬇	⬇
(C)	**(F)**	**(G)**	**(Am)**
Red	**yellow**	**green**	**blue**
⬇	⬇	⬇	⬇
(C)	**(F)**	**(G)**	**(C)**
That's	**the**	**switch-**	**eroo!**
⬇	⬇	⬇	⬇

FUN FACT

Ukuleles tend to have a figure-eight shape
and look similar to an acoustic guitar.

10-Strum Challenge

The way to improve on ukulele is to become a smooth strummer. Once you've learned the 4 dot chords, you'll be ready to play most songs. So now, let's focus on your strumming. Try each of the 10 strumming patterns below. Then try all of the patterns again using F G and Am instead of C.

Count-in: 1, 2, 3, 4 between each pattern.

1. Down/Down/Down-Up/Down

C	C	C	C	X 4
Down	Down	Down-Up	Down	
⬇	⬇	⬇⬆	⬇	

2. Down/Down/Down-Up/Down-Up

C	C	C	C	X 4
Down	Down	Down-Up	Down-Up	
⬇	⬇	⬇⬆	⬇⬆	

3. Down/Down-Up/Down/Down-Up

C	C	C	C	X 4
Down	Down-Up	Down	Down-Up	
⬇	⬇⬆	⬇	⬇⬆	

4. Down-Up/Down-Up/Down-Up/Down

C	C	C	C	X 4
Down-Up	Down-Up	Down-Up	Down	
⬇⬆	⬇⬆	⬇⬆	⬇	

5. Down/Down/Hold/Up-Down-Up

C	C	👏	C	X 4
Down	Down	Hold	Up-Down-Up	
⬇	⬇		⬆⬇⬆	

6. Down/Down-Up/Hold/Up-Down

Down	Down-Up	Hold	Up-Down	X 4
⬇	⬇⬆		⬆⬇	

7. Down/Down-Up/Hold/Up-Down-Up

Down	Down-Up	Hold	Up-Down-Up	X 4
⬇	⬇⬆		⬆⬇⬆	

8. Down/Down/Hold/Down

Down	Down	Hold	Down	X 4
⬇	⬇		⬇	

9. Down/Hold/Down/Hold

Down	Hold	Down	Hold	X 4
⬇		⬇		

10. Down-Up/Down-Up/Down-Up/Down

Down-Up	Down-Up	Down-Up	Down	X 4
⬇⬆	⬇⬆	⬇⬆	⬇	

The Song Recipe

Have you been hoping to create your own songs on the ukulele? Songwriting is my favorite part of being a musician! I'm going to share my recipe for making a song. Here it is:

- **4 chords or less**

- **1 strumming pattern (you can use ideas from the "10-Strum Challenge" on page 76)**

- **Your own lyrics (words)**

Directions

Play at a medium speed a couple of times. Then perform for a friend, family member . . . or pet. (I'm pretty sure my dog loves my songs!)

Here's an example:

LINE 1

C	C	G	C
I	like	to	dream
↓	↓	↓	↓

LINE 2

C	C	G	C
of	yummy	ice	cream!
↓	↓	↓	↓

Write Your Own Song!

Song Title: _____

By: _____ Date: _____

LINE 1

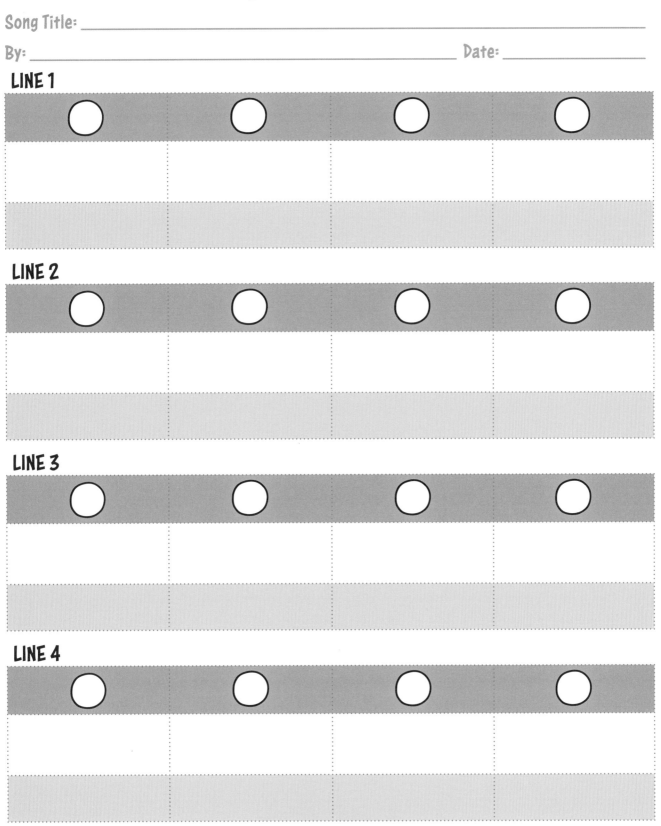

LINE 2

LINE 3

LINE 4

Song Title: _____

By: _____ Date: _____

LINE 1

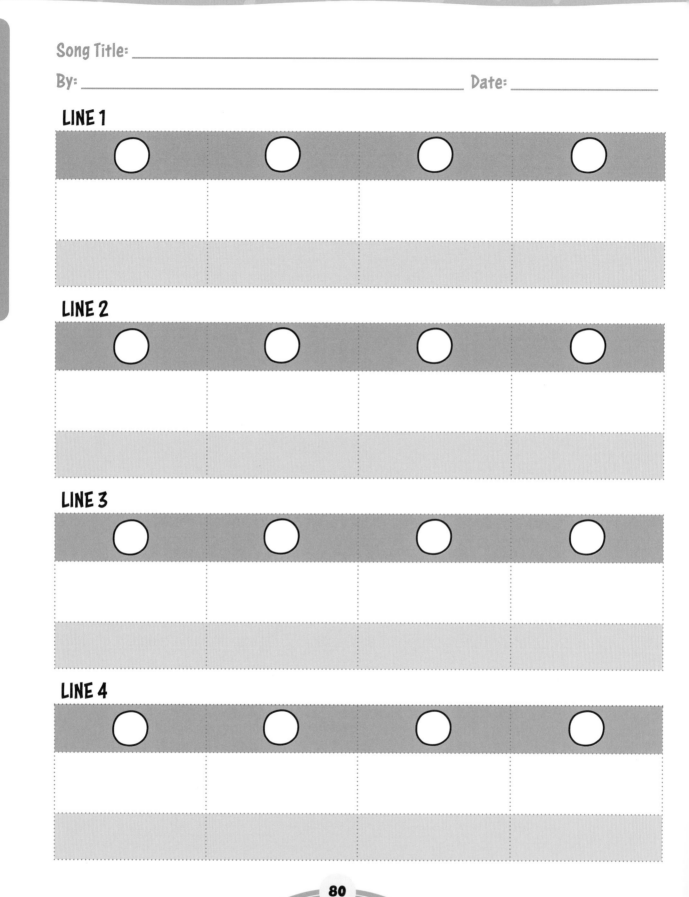

LINE 2

LINE 3

LINE 4

Song Title: _____

By: _____ Date: _____

LINE 1

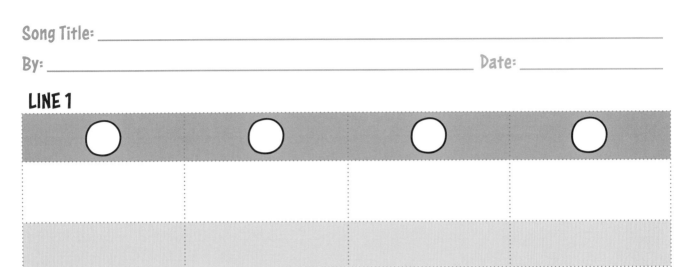

LINE 2

LINE 3

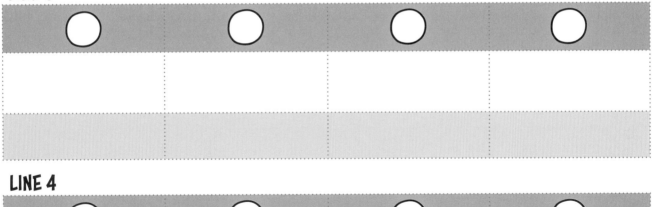

LINE 4

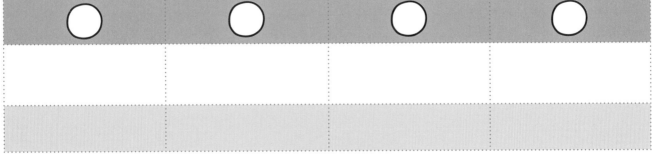

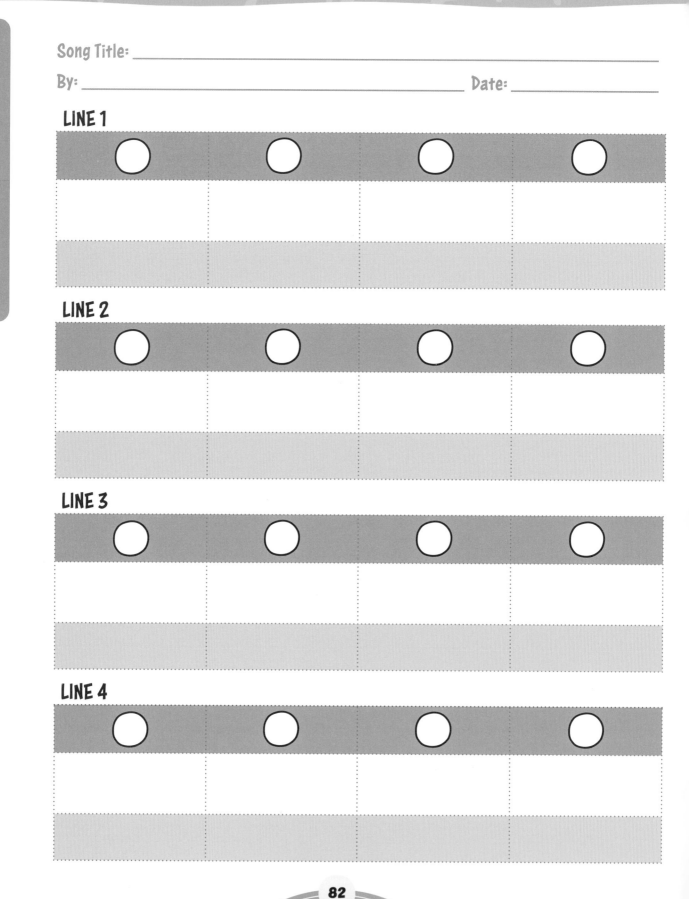

Song Title: _____

By: _____ Date: _____

LINE 1

LINE 2

LINE 3

LINE 4

Song Title: _____

By: _____ Date: _____

LINE 1

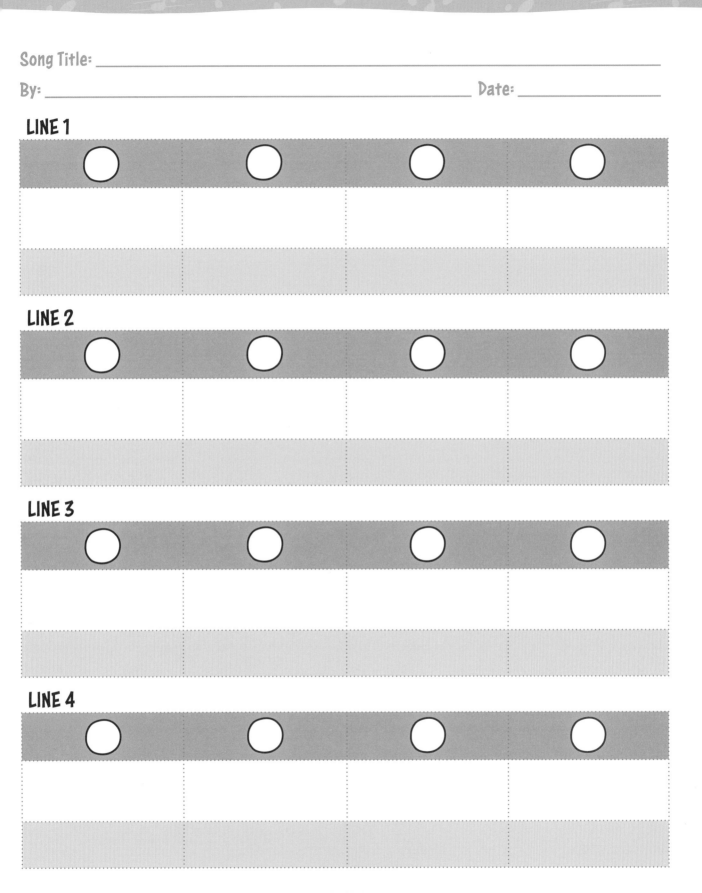

LINE 2

LINE 3

LINE 4

Song Title: _____

By: _____ Date: _____

LINE 1

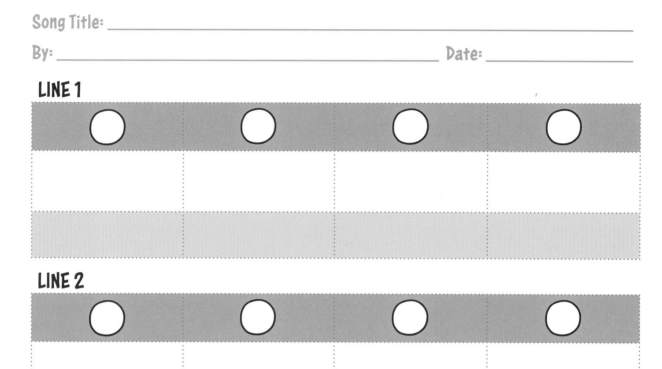

LINE 2

LINE 3

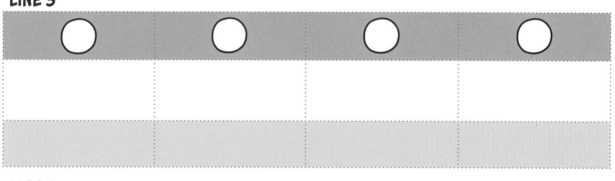

LINE 4

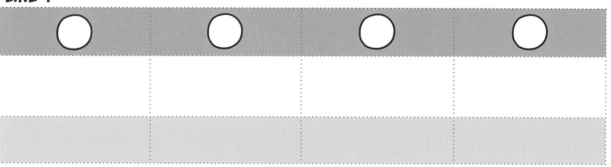

Song Title: _____

By: _____ Date: _____

LINE 1

LINE 2

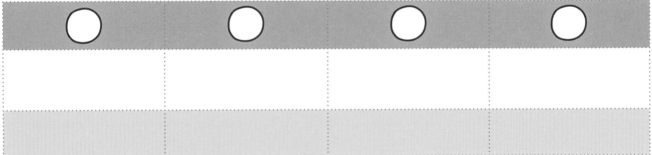

LINE 3

LINE 4

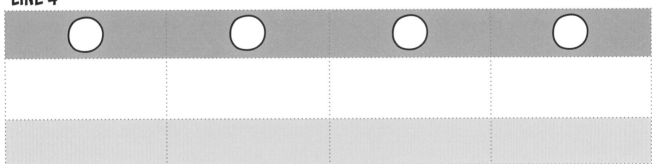

Song Title: _____

By: _____ Date: _____

LINE 1

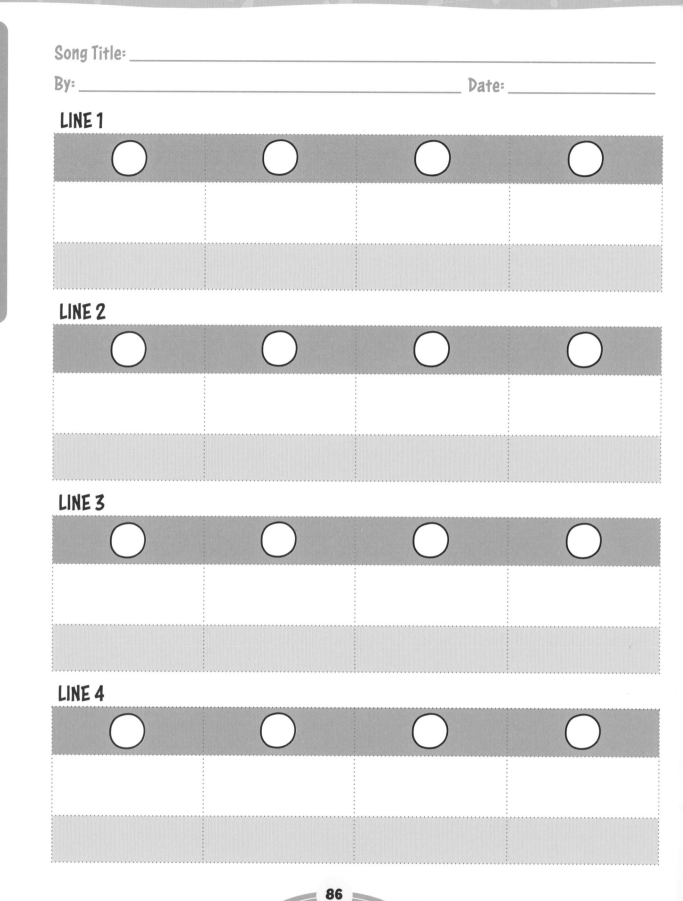

LINE 2

LINE 3

LINE 4

Song Title: _____

By: _____ Date: _____

LINE 1

LINE 2

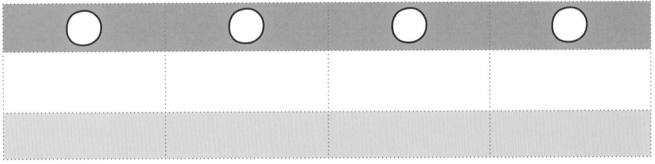

LINE 3

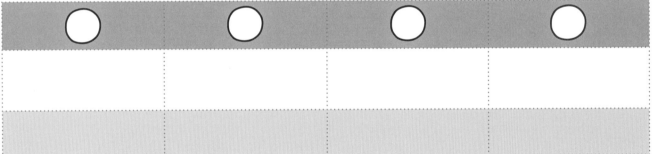

LINE 4

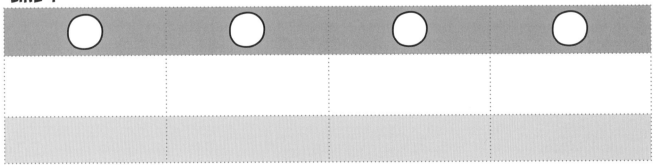

Song Title: _____

By: _____ Date: _____

LINE 1

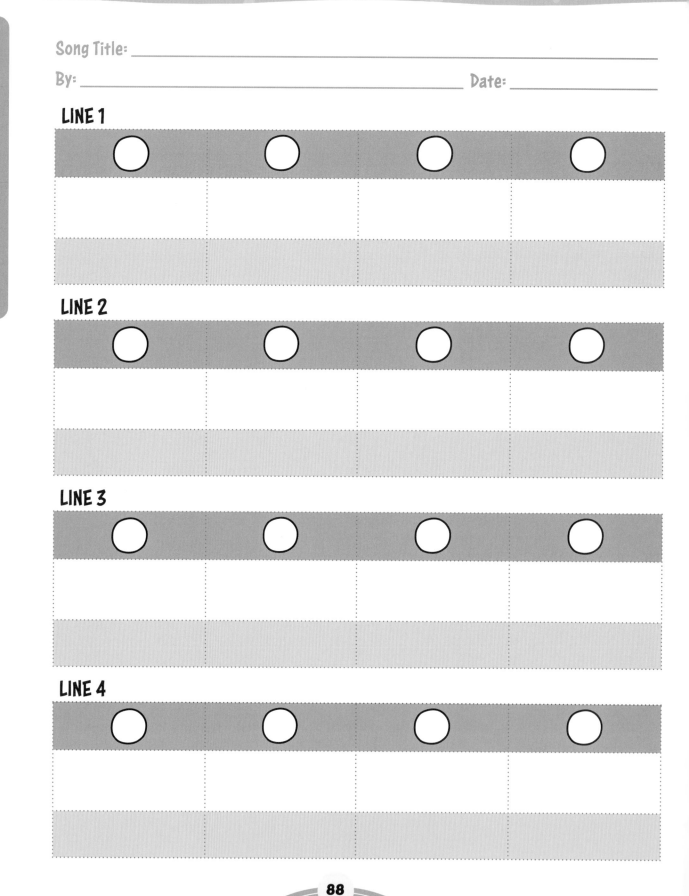

LINE 2

LINE 3

LINE 4

Song Title: _____

By: _____ Date: _____

LINE 1

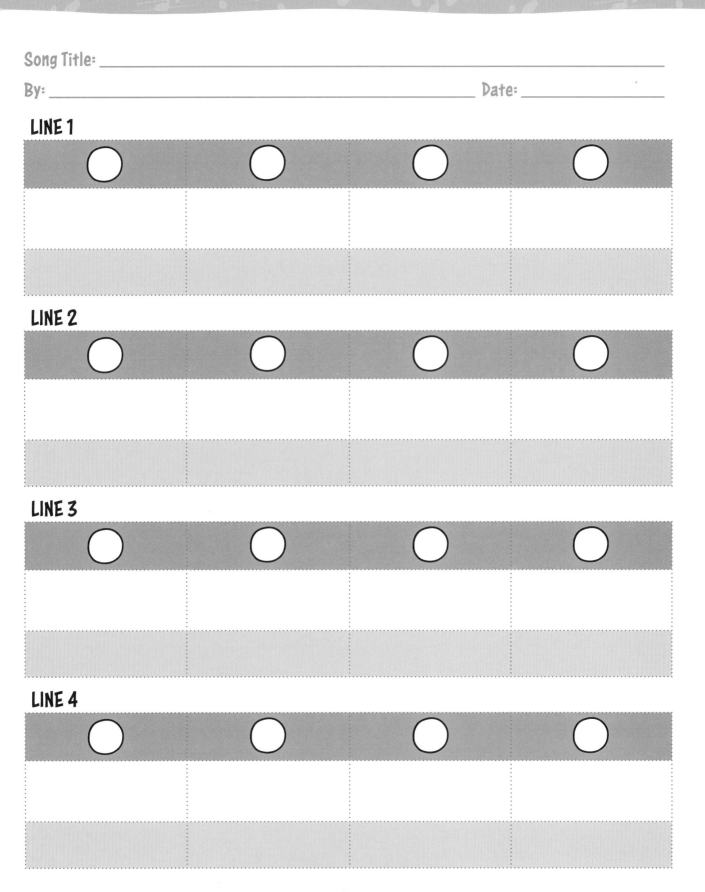

LINE 2

LINE 3

LINE 4

Practice Journey

Try practicing about 4 times a week for 10 minutes (or so)!

Each time you practice, fill in the box with your own "sticker" by drawing something fun. Decide how you'll celebrate when you reach the ukulele at the end! Then you get to start the journey all over again.

START

END

START

END

START

END

START

END

Index

About the Author

Emily Arrow is an award-winning children's songwriter with more than ten years of experience working with children in music education. An official Kala Brand Music Co. artist, picture book author, and popular YouTube personality, Emily and her ukulele named Bow foster a love for literacy and music.

Her *Storytime Singalong, Volumes 1–3* include #1 songs on SiriusXM's Kids' Place Live and have received recognitions of The Lennon Award, National Parenting Products Award, Nashville Scene's Best Local Kid's Entertainer, and Parents' Choice Gold Award.

Emily's debut as a picture book author is *Studio: A Place for Art to Start*, which celebrates spaces for creativity to grow. She is also the composer and writer of the library series *My Feelings, My Choices*.

A proud graduate of Berklee College of Music, Emily began writing for children during her time as a K–6 music educator in Los Angeles. She is certified in Orff Shulwerk, an approach in music education for young musicians. During her years teaching, Emily found that her "contemporary" approach to music instruction helped her to connect with children and inspired them to become excited about learning to play music.

Emily and Bow tour bookstores, festivals, and venues around the country to share the ukulele magic. When she's not on the road, Emily splits her time between Nashville, Los Angeles, and Portland, Oregon. Visit *www.EmilyArrow.com* to learn more and sing along!

Chord Stickers

Make learning to play easier with chord stickers! Using the illustration on this page, place chord stickers on the fretboard of your ukulele to help your fingers find the right spot when playing. As the stickers wear out, simply replace them or leave them off as you memorize the chords.

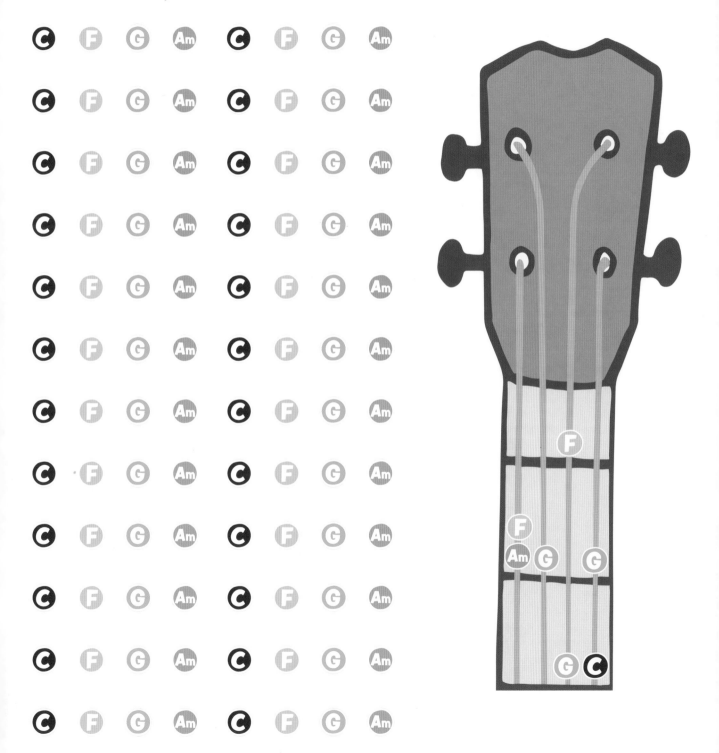